T0380773

Copyright © 2015 by Clara. 696908

ISBN: Softcover   978-1-4990-9344-5
       EBook   978-1-4990-9345-2

All rights reserved. No part of this book may be
reproduced or transmitted in any form or by
any means, electronic or mechanical, including
photocopying, recording, or by any information
storage and retrieval system, without permission
in writing from the copyright owner.

Print information available on the last page.

Rev. date: 03/23/2015

To order additional copies of this book, contact:
Xlibris
0800-056-3182
www.xlibrispublishing.co.uk
Orders@ Xlibrispublishing.co.uk

Contents

Untitled – Mother
親和

Today of all day's, a day of changes.

The day that things were not the same anymore, the day that made you feel, as if nothing was real.

If the clock was turn back what could you do, these are only thoughts.

Thoughts that make you wonder and feel sad.

It's a sad day for you; only you know how you feel.

Cry if you must; for that will release the pain in your heart.

Don't forget that this day of all day's was the happiest day; for someone who loved you so much and who wish could be there for you.

She is with you; you don't have to look for her anymore. She is within you.

Please try not to feel sad; for she is free and happy.

She will always be there for you in spirit. She will always watch over you.

I am sure she wants you to be happy and not feel sad because she has gone.

She creates the path for you to lead your life; a wonderful life for you; so don't fall apart now.

Don't let her teaching and guidance go to waste.

The bound of a mother to her son is forever even if the chain is broken.

Remember she has gone through another path.

She is creating and waiting for when you will be part of her chain again.

She hasn't really gone forever; she is waiting for her chain to be joined again.

This is your time to make a choice; only you can do that.

I am your friend but one day I might not be here too.

Things can't be forever; things have to change; so has to give the other things a chance to experience what we have.

Be happy within yourself; only you can do that.

Friends Forever & In Spirit!!!

親和

Summer Love

親和

Summer is here now and the year has gone by me.

A year today is when my life fell apart.

I have tried so hard to forget the pain and misery that has put me on hold (for some time).

The ray of sunshine this time round has made me realise; that time has not stopped.

For time is moving on; slowly by slowly.

I am coming to terms with everything.

The future seems brighter again.

I feel destined to achieve my goals again.

The spark that once made me glow as returned.

How lucky that I have come through this and survived on my own.

Being afraid is the only thing that stops you, from having the strength and courage to survive.

Feeling like a puppet when every string is pulled because it brings happiness and security.

Only to realise that the person pulling your strings is no longer there.

You have no idea why that is.

All you know is that your strings are cut and you don't know what to do.

The sadness of love or believing that you are in love with someone.

Only to realise that the feelings are not the same.

A mistake we all do at some point.

How easily we are deceived by words; that sounds beautiful and meaningful.

Promise of love with no meaning when it's not truly from the heart.

Friends Forever & In Spirit!!!

Believe In You
親和

When everything and everyone are against you don't lose hope; believe in your inner strength and power.

This will see you through the nightmare, the end and the darkness you feel now.

If you give up what you have achieved.

What have you done except given up on yourself and the one that would die for you.

You have to believe in you, feel your inner power and be stronger than you have ever been before.

Life is not easy; that's no reason to give up and hide away when everything, everyone are closing in towards you.

Look for the doors that will bring wondrous and new adventurous into your life.

The doors you open or the solutions you find might not be the right one for now.

But because you have made that little more effort it keeps your spirits up until you finally stop searching.

Only your fear and not believing in you will prevent you from looking beyond what you see in front of you.

Everything that goes wrong must have a solution for making it right again.

Believe in you and you will find the right solution for what seems to be your worst nightmare.

Friends Forever & In Spirit!!!

Let Me Be There For You

親和

I want to be part of your life but you seem to shut me out. I want to help because I care for you.

Why wouldn't you let me be there for you.

You don't have to feel that you own me or feel obliged to return the favour.

Just let me be there for you, to see you through the hard times and the bad times.

I can't stand by knowing that you are confused and unhappy with life.

Let me be there for you, to see you through the trouble times in your life.

There are no strings or drawbacks; don't shut me out; tell me and let me help you.

You are part of my life and I can't carry on with just a part of me.

You are my strength; why wouldn't you let me be there for you.

Pride and respect doesn't have to change; you need help and I want to help.

My feeling for you is more than that of love; we were destined to meet and to guide each other through life.

You are the missing puzzle that I have being looking for in my life.

Let me be there for you until you find your missing puzzle (Just let me be there for you).

You are uncertain of what's happening around you.

You are trying very hard to take hold but each time you get closer it's gone.

Take hold of my hand; let me guide you back; for there is hope and happiest if we search together.

No need to be afraid; for we will be united if only you let be there for you.

How can I help you if you wouldn't talk. How can I be there when you wouldn't tell me to stay. How can I give you encouragement when you wouldn't say how you feel.

What can I do when you wouldn't help me so that I can help you when you are feeling down.

Please let me be there for you when you are feeling low (Just let me be there for you).

My heart and soul is low when you are feeling this way. Just talk to me and I will be there for you.

Friends Forever & In Spirit!!!

Words

親和

What are words that have no meaning. What are words when it's not the truth. What are words when it's just an expression of your voice.

Words; only words can hurt when there are lies or used to make you unhappy.

Sometimes promises are made from words that sounds and make you feel good at the time.

Then only to let you down when you need it the most.

We are fool's for believing in words especially when there are lies in the end.

How can we be sure that the words being use now to make us believe and feel save is the truth.

The world is still moving and everyone has to keep up because there is no escaping for any of us.

The world is life for us and so are words.

Pain, tears, broken heart, misery, laughter, joyfulness, friendship and happiness are built on words of truth and lie.

Nobody can be absolutely perfect so how can we accept words to have it's true meaning when used.

There is always someone who will disappoint you and so can words.

Life is sometimes a pain and so can words. Life can be confusing and so can words.

There is a never ending use of words and it's part of our life.

Friends Forever & In Spirit!!!

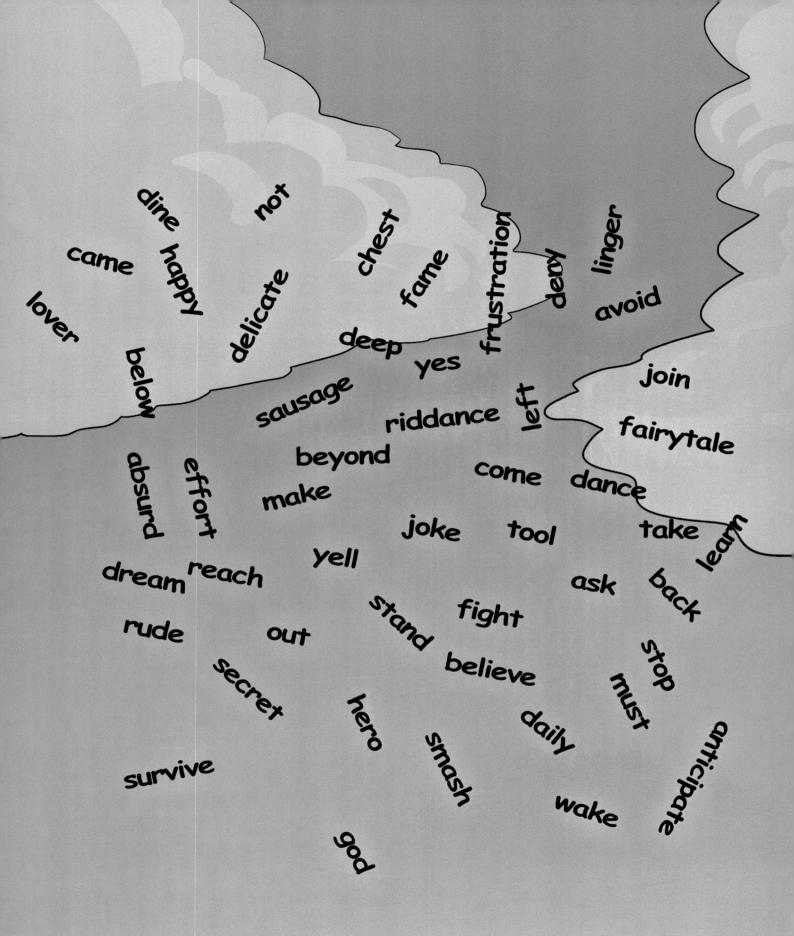

Heavenly
親和

Oh heavenly father you have always watched over me and guided me through the confusing times in my life. Your force and your encouragement have given me the drive that is needed to overcome my problems.

How I have taken you for granted and not believed that you were close by me all this time.

Your forgiveness is what I should be asking for.

All I seem to do is keep on demanding and praying for your help constantly.

You have made me what I am today; a good and kind person; please do not let that change.

Make me stronger to overcome those who try to make me miserable, hurt me and just use me.

For in their eyes I am just an object that has no feelings and cannot speak out.

Only you know my whole life and what has being happening.

What chapter of my life I am up too.

There is no need for me to tell you how I have been feeling because apart from me knowing.

I know that you have taken every step with me since the start of my life.

Oh heavenly father am I the last of my kind or am I in a different world from everyone else.

Friends Forever & In Spirit!!!

The Pain The Pain
親和

How do you stop the pain; this feeling which hurts so deeply when you are longing to be together but can't be together.

It hurts so bad, it's so sad and you want to die to stop the pain.

You know it hurts; you can see it in their eyes, they can see it in your eyes too.

How to stop the pain; you can't let go but you want to let go.

Walk away; how when you can't move, won't move because you are in love.

The pain draws you in each time when you are close to one another.

I know you want me as much as I want you.

I know you need me as much as I need you.

I want to give in and be close to you.

I want to hold you as much as you want to hold me; to make the pain stop; to make everything better.

You have a hold on me as much as I have with you.

You pull me towards you as much as I do to you.

I feel what you feeling because it's happening to me too.

The pain, The pain; how can it stop when it's like the air we are breathing.

I need to come up for air and space.

The pain, The Pain; what could it be.

Why does it hurt as much as it does.

Make it stop; why doesn't it stop.

What makes it hurts so badly. The pain, The pain.

Friends Forever & In Spirit!!!

Hopefully In Love
親和

Love me forever, love me forever and I shall be yours forever.

Hold me and I shall be yours forever.

Kiss me and I shall be yours forever.

For, I am yours and hopefully in love with you.

I have lost control because I am hopefully in love, hopefully in love.

My emotions have taken over; telling me to open up and to trust you.

Should I or shan't I; only time will tell.

The way you make me feel is unreal; like nothing I have experience before.

This could be the real thing.

When I am with you; I am floating in a dream world of make believe.

Wishing never to return to reality.

Things are not forever.

I know I am; hopefully in love, hopefully in love.

It's too late to stop or run; for I am yours forever; I yearn.

All I ask of you; is to love me forever and I wouldn't hurt you; I yearn.

Love is strange; like nothing matters when you're hopefully in love, hopefully in love.

The sound of your heart beating fast and skipping a beat whilst dreaming of your love.

Waiting and ready to explode when you are far away from each other.

Love is strange when you're hopefully in love, hopefully in love, hopefully in love.

Friends Forever & In Spirit!!!

It Doesn't Have To Be Hard, Saying Goodbye
親和

Time has come closer than expected; it doesn't have to be hard or difficult. Just say goodbye.

We had a great time and shared a lot together; let's remember all the good times.

You are hurting and so am I; why prolong the situation.

You are unhappy and so am I.

It's time to let go and make a new start.

Together we may not be but friendship doesn't have to stop.

It doesn't have to be hard saying goodbye; saying goodbye but not forever.

Don't shut me out of your life because I don't feel the same way about you now.

I still care for you. I will always care and look after you.

Our life might be different and heading towards a different path.

Let's not forget the moments we had together; there were good times.

It doesn't have to be hard saying goodbye; saying goodbye but not forever.

Always remember me when you need a friend.

I will always be your friend no matter how much it hurt's now.

Within time; I hope you will consider me a friend that will always be there for you.

Saying goodbye, saying goodbye; it doesn't have to be hard.

Friends Forever & In Spirit!!!

I Am Drawn To You Like A Magnet
親和

The time never seems right there is always something happening.

I should be upset but I am not; like a magnet I am drawn to you.

Unable to break free because we are one; our soul and heart is tuned together; like a magnet I am drawn to you.

The current that flows in me when I am with you is like electric shocks; electrifying in me but it's harmless.

For I feel weak for a second then the current seems to join us together. Then I am strong; like a magnet I am drawn to you.

I am not afraid to show my emotions now trust and honesty is what bound us closer.

You don't have to be afraid to ask me or tell me something; just say what you truly feel.

Like a magnet I am drawn to you.

When you are sad I can feel it; when you are upset I can feel it and when you don't want to talk I can sense it.

I am here for you as a friend and for comfort so don't feel that I wouldn't understand your feelings.

Like a magnet I am drawn to you.

I know that you wouldn't take advantage of me; wouldn't take me for granted and try hard not to hurt me. So be calm with yourself; for I know it's hard but we will try.

I will be your strength and you will be mine. We are linked together forever. Like a magnet I am drawn to you.

Each day is a new beginning together we will look to it and be strong for one another.

I love you with all my heart, that's all I can offer you for now.

When the time comes for us to part don't be afraid to tell me and I wouldn't be afraid to tell you.

Apart we may be but like a magnet I will always be drawn to you.

Friends Forever & In Spirit!!!

Where Do You Turn

親和

Where do you turn, where do you turn when friends don't want to know; lover seem too busy to care and family seem to be too demanding all the time.

There is no way/where for you to go.

Pain and sadness fills your heart; loneliness and confusion weigh on your mind.

Where do you turn?

Help; who can help you; no one except you.

Look for the door; the door that will lead you to a better place.

Just keep looking for it's closer than you think.

There is always an opportunity if you search for it.

Where do you turn, where do you turn.

Broken promises; broken heart and too many disappointments.

How do you cope when everything is hard?

You want to let go but you keep holding on; why?

So many questions with no answers for them.

Where do you turn?

Hope, believing and time is all that you can give to yourself.

You can be the friend to guide yourself back on track.

Lover's will come and go but family will always be demanding.

You will cope and feel stronger in time; for there is no place to hide.

Where do you turn, where do you turn.

Friends Forever & In Spirit!!!

M . J
親和

How the world can turn against you. The world was yours to conquer but now it's crumbling beneath you.

What have you done to deserve this; what are you left with.

To start again, is out of the question. For it's taken you a life time to achieve what you had.

Brave, Heroic, Icon, Idol is what you have to be.

For you are the greatest history; history can't be forgotten.

Why be judged when you have nothing to hide.

This is a hustle world we live in.

Being judged for what you have done; regardless may be good or bad; we all have to pay in the end.

The history that you have created shouldn't be forgotten.

In the eyes of many you are still the greatest and the best of all time.

Darkness does fall on us at some stage in our life.

You can make the light shine again for yourself.

Think back to the past for there has been so much you have missed out on.

The time has come for you to move on and to stop trying to make up for it.

Live and act within now instead of the past.

Everyone has to grow-up some day; make today your day.

Look in the mirror; see for yourself you are not a child.

In your; mind you feel like a little child and you want to act like a child.

There is nothing wrong with that as long as you can be focus with the present time and not the past.

Friends Forever & In Spirit!!!

Don't Feel That You Are Alone
親和

Don't feel that you are alone.

I have endure the feelings that you are experiencing so don't feel that you are alone.

It's hard to express your feelings when all you want to do is keep them to yourself.

There is no reason to hide or to feel that no one understands; that nobody could ever feel the way you do.

You are wrong; for I have been there and I am sure that you will find many others.

So don't feel that you are alone.

You feel you can't trust anyone; who can you trust when you don't feel as if you can trust yourself.

So who do you trust to tell?

Just tell someone; for you will not be alone.

You don't have to be afraid, you don't have to be afraid; there is no reason to think the whole world is coming down on you.

Don't feel that you are alone.

It's hard; you will cope and never give up believing in you.

Don't feel that you are alone.

Friends Forever & In Spirit!!!

You Have Made Me Fall In Love

親和

Somehow you have made me fall in love with you. I am drawn to you like a magnet unable to control my feelings and actions.

When you look at me I skip a beat. When you stare at me I go weak. When you smile I smile with you.

You have made me fall in love with you.

I have never told anyone I love you. I have always kept it a secret and you weren't supposed to know how I truly feel.

You have made me fall in love with you.

You stand looking at me with a smile wondering what to say. You have drawn me towards you with your charms, wit, intelligent and humorous mood.

Every time you stare; I feel weak, dreamy and hollow in my heart.

You have made me fall in love with you.

I try to control my feelings, to show no emotions but it's an act. My feelings are stronger than they have ever been before.

I know that I am in love.

For you have made me fall in love, fallen in love with you.

Friends Forever & In Spirit!!!

Truly The Real Thing

親和

I don't know where or how to start, I don't know what to say and I don't know how blinded I was not to see.

So many times you tried to tell me and to show me but I still couldn't understand.

You brought happiness when I was sad and alone, you saw what I couldn't see in me, you knew what I did not or couldn't understand.

At times you must have thought that I was teasing or playing a cruel game with you because nobody surely cannot know or see that it was truly the real thing.

Being 16 going onto 17, the in-between of childish behaviours coming to an end and trying to understand life and yourself; daydreaming, falling in love and falling out of love, every week, every month with everything and everyone that looks nice or cute.

Picturing a life with someone in your head and missing out on truly the real thing when it's clearly in front of you to see, to hold, to cherish and to be happy.

How could I have let you go as my heart split in half, a pain that I have never felt before until that moment I said 'No'.

My heart told me it was wrong and that I shall regret this day forever, for the rest of my life and that I shall not be able to live a happier life again because this was going to be the greatest mistake that I could ever do.

In a moment, a short moment in my thoughts, a quick flash in front of me, shows the unhappiest of a broken heart and the unknown with you which seemed to be scarier because I wasn't ready to change. I was not ready to change with truly the real thing.

You knew and seem to understand that I was not ready; you wanted to be close until the time I could see what's truly the real thing.

How I could have hurt you so much, how clueless I could have been, why it has taken me so long, so long to see, to see what I couldn't see in myself and in you.

A love that needs no word; a love of soul mates; a love of true happiness; a love that makes you a better person; a love that scares you because it's unknown; a love that makes you behave in ways that can't be explain in words because it feels like you are in a daze of a wonderful, wonderful dream; a love that hurts between us because it's never balance at the same time.

How could I have let you go when truly the real thing.

So many years has gone by, if only I knew what I could clearly see now I would have never let you go; never let you go.

I dream and I hope that we could have a second chance; a second chance for what is truly, the real thing.

Friends Forever & In Spirit!!!

Why Am I Here
親和

Ask the question why am I here. Small things, little things, simply things, insufficient things mean a lot and makes a different.

You can't see it but others can and it means a lot. It touches them to move on and overcome their struggle and pain.

You are here, that's what matters, no questions, no understanding it. There is a reason for everything, it doesn't have to make sense and you don't have to see it to understand why.

Why am I here, questions; questions. There is no answers just be grateful it's your time to make a different.

Why am I here because you matter to complete the circle of a life or more.

Why am I here, questions; questions. You are loved always and important although it doesn't feel like it.

Can't you see how you have touched others, can't you see how happy your life is, can't you see who truly cares and matters.

A smile opens their happiness.

A touch lightens their life.

A kind word means more than you can imagine.

You are wonderful, you are an angel and you are a star beyond words.

Don't go; stay.

Friends Forever & In Spirit!!!

My Soulmate
親和

Why can't I find you, why can't I feel you by my side, why have I not met you, why am I at a lost and why am I alone.

Have I met you but didn't feel the sparks.

Have I touch you but no connection of emotions.

Have I spoken to you but no signs showing or telling me you are my soulmate.

Have our path cross but nothing to link us together.

Am I doomed to walk this life alone because my soulmate is no longer in this life circle?

Am I to search until eternally for my soulmate.

Am I to continue hiding away because it hurts?

Shall I open my heart again for my soulmate.

Shall I hope again for my soulmate.

Shall I be in a happy medium for my soulmate.

Shall I believe my soulmate will appear in this life circle.

Give me strength to hold on.

Give me time to adjust to reality that my soulmate will not cross my life circle.

Give me a glance into the future how I can find my soulmate.

Friends Forever & In Spirit!!!

Random Thoughts 1
親和

You enter when there was no hope left. You enter when there was darkness. You enter when I gave up.

Where do I start to tell you that only you have made me happy and smile again.

No more tears, no more loneliness; now things are bright once again.

Only you, only you, could make me feel this way again.

So far away from each other but somehow we were brought together just as we needed to be loved.

To feel save, to feel that we belong and that we are not alone.

****

Show a bit of love; show some emotional and you are hook.

People can change; unfortunately not the people in your life.

They know which buttons to push; how to manipulate your kind nature.

Breakaway; Breakaway that's all you can do.

It's hard and you will be alone but happier.

****

Hearing or being told something that you can't contemplate in the moment.

Being in a trance; here but not here.

Feeling an uplifting free sensation feeling.

A kiss paralysing you; here but not here.

A joy that's fully with fast snap shots flowing and racing within the past and present.

The fear but calm in the moment; you are not alone.

The reach close but never coming to you.

Friends Forever & In Spirit!!!

Random Thoughts 2
親和

Believing in you is all you can really count on. Nobody is going to really stand up for you. Nobody is going to help or be there for you when it really counts.

So maybe you don't belong in their crowd; is that anyway to treat someone just because they don't belong.

I don't belong in your crowd; I don't belong in your crowd.

I have don't know harm but still I am the one that's being treated weird.

****

Things happen to change you. You see things and want to act upon these things out of anger, disappointment, frustration and fright.

You can't always change what's happening but instead learn from it. Evolve and be better and do things you know in your heart is right. These are the things to hold on too. These are the things to remember and pray to always be who you are without changing to someone else. A person you can't recognise, believe in and trust.

Don't change me, let me be strong to cope and handle the situation.

Don't change me, allow me to always remember so that I can avoid going down the wrong path.

Don't change me because I truly like who I am someone with a kind heart and still in-touch with society. Someone still pure as a child who is seeing and learning new things every day.

Don't change me because I am a believer of society has a magically place for all, to treat one another with love, kindness and respect.

Our past holds so much. Events occurs which we wish to forget. Incidents we want to hold on too forever like love, kindness and support that were there or not.

In our present lives we are trying to move on, find what we are still seeking and sometimes not sure if it's the right path. There are always doubts when you choice a new path.

The future is always down to you. You have to make it happen with help or no help along the way. The unknown is scary but you can already picture the happy ending so work for it. Follow the right path and remain true to one's self.

Friends Forever & In Spirit!!!

Gossip & Lies
親和

That's just sticks and stones, sticks and stones.

Gossip & lies, how lethal and harmful these words have on our life's.

People can be jealous, people can be envious, people can be heartless; people can pretend to be one thing in your face and then their true nature behind your back.

These are the ones who like to Gossip & Lies, Gossip & Lies.

Always pretending, they are your friends, they have got your back, whilst all the time stabbing you in the back with their Gossip & Lies, Gossip & Lies.

True friends what a joke when really they are your adversaries – yeah your foes.

They want what you have, they can't understand why it's yours, why you are the one with the luck, good things etc… etc… on and on. Yeah; what a joke!!!.

You worked hard for what you do have. There is no luck, you are kind and treat everyone fairly so good things will happen and bad things will happen. These are facts not Gossip & Lies, Gossip & Lies.

You know better, you can see through them, their eyes are like looking into a mirror with their Gossip & Lies, Gossip & Lies that has no end.

They hearts and fake smiles is plain and clear to see, it's all a game for them. A game they must win to feel power and satisfaction in hurting you, bring you down, waiting to see the sadness in your face. They will keep pushing and feeling more and more confident with their Gossip & Lies, Gossip & Lies.

When the time comes, when the time is right you will know. Don't fall for their Gossip & Lies, no matter how hard you try to show it's not true. They will always find ways to keep up their Gossip & Lies, Gossip & Lies.

Proof, yeah, evidences and facts; should be realistic facts but it's not because it's all based on their feelings. What a joke!!!.

Feelings based on what, oh yeah Gossip & Lies, Gossip & Lies.

Great way to remove your nemesis, great way to feel superior, great way to take credit for others efforts and work, when your only skills are Gossip & Lies, Gossip & Lies.

Shall I feel sorry for them, no totally a waste of time, to give in to the bullies of the world, sad individuals who seek others talents to claim as their own or put them down with their Gossip & Lies, Gossip & Lies.

You don't need people to tell you how good you are. You know, you can feel it in you.

Don't hold back, believe in you, more than ever to achieve and to do what you are supposed to do.

Spite and jealously is what's it's really all about. They see what you can't see or what you wouldn't truly believe you can do. Be brave, don't let fear hold you back, don't let doubts hold you back and especially don't let Gossip & Lies, Gossip & Lies.

Don't let these things …

Confuse you, discourage you from your dreams, your hopes, your wishes, your hard work, your believes and who you are.

Fight the Gossip & Lies, Gossip & Lies.

The true way, is by doing and being you.

No need to change, no need to bring yourself down to their level, no need to verbally or physically fight back. Being you and doing what you have always done is enough for now.

Yeah, it's hard, yeah you want to cry, yeah you want to hide, yeah you want it all to go away, yeah you wish it never happened, yeah you wish you had a true friend, yeah you wish you can talk and share how you are feeling, yeah you wish you were dead or never born.

The list is endless so stop, take charge, feel and listen, really listen to the whisper in you, desperately trying to fight, stand-up for you, giving you the strength and power to rise above it all.

For words can't hurt you, words can't really break you, words can be cruel just like some people whose talent in the world is Gossip & Lies, Gossip & Lies.

These are people who are useless really, no real talent, bullies, wishing to have what you have and wishing they can change their lives.

Yep, it's sad and a lonely place for anyone to be. You should feel sorry for them and you should thank them for opening your eyes.

For you are on the next level beyond their grasp because in time you will be where you are supposed to be whilst they will be struck in their web of Gossip & Lies, Gossip & Lies for eternally.

No need to list their names, no need to give them a platform to be famous. Just list the alphabet because we all know an A,B,C,D,E,F,G,H,I … J,K,L,M,N,O,P…Q,R,S,T,U,V,W,X,Y,Zee

Don't let them bring you down. You know who they are …friends, family, work colleagues, your boss, work friends, school friends, strangers that you don't know but they say they know you, so call hang-on, so calls wanabes, so call know it all, so call look at me, so call I am drop dead gorgeous, so call everyone like me, so call you can't live without me, so call you are nothing without me, so call I made you.

Yeah, some of it might be true but most of it is Gossip & Lies, Gossip & Lies.

Friends Forever & In Spirit!!!